TODAY'S WEATHER:
RAINING - CATS & DOGS
MAX: 1 PER OWNER.

SPECIAL EDITION

CONTENTS: 80 PAGES
FEATURING GARFIELD'S EXPLOITS.

The Garfield Times

© 1978 United Feature Syndicate, Inc.

Published by Ravette Limited

APRIL FOOL'S DAY

THIS IS YOUR LIFE

BY: JIM DAVIS

ℛℛ
Ravette London

This edition first published by
Ravette Limited 1988

Printed and bound in Great Britain
for Ravette Limited,
3 Glenside Estate, Star Road, Partridge Green,
Horsham, Sussex RH13 8RA
by The Guernsey Press Company Limited,
Guernsey, Channel Islands

ISBN 1 85304 024 X

THIS IS YOUR LIFE

BY: JIM DAVIS

Garfield has his face splashed all over the front page today in the latest edition of this famous cat's lifestyle.

The inside story is outside for all to enjoy. The following pages feature the exclusive pictures of a career spanning nine lifetimes with no end in sight.

You can share some of the hilarious experiences with Garfield as he travels through his most unusual life in the usual Garfield manner.

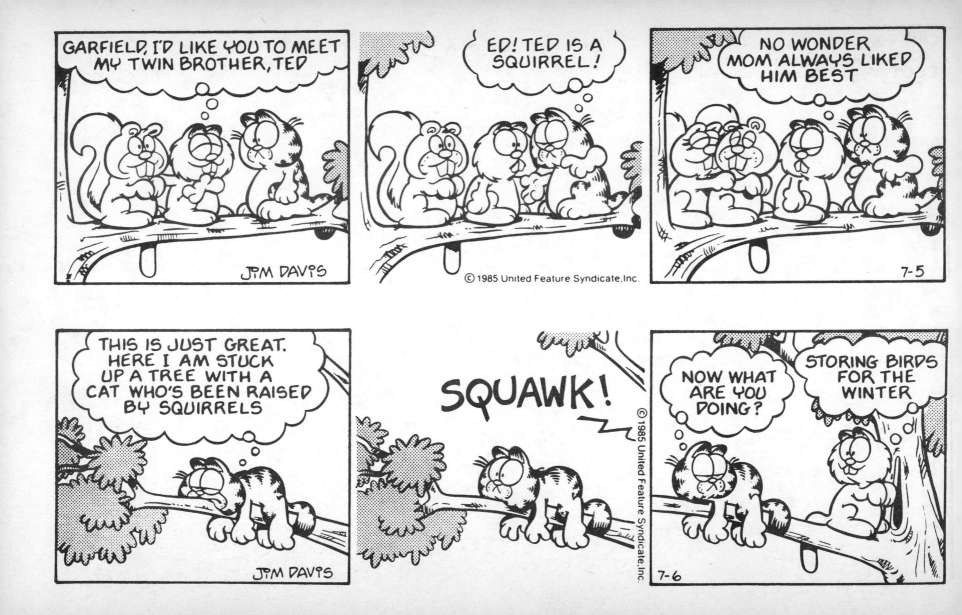

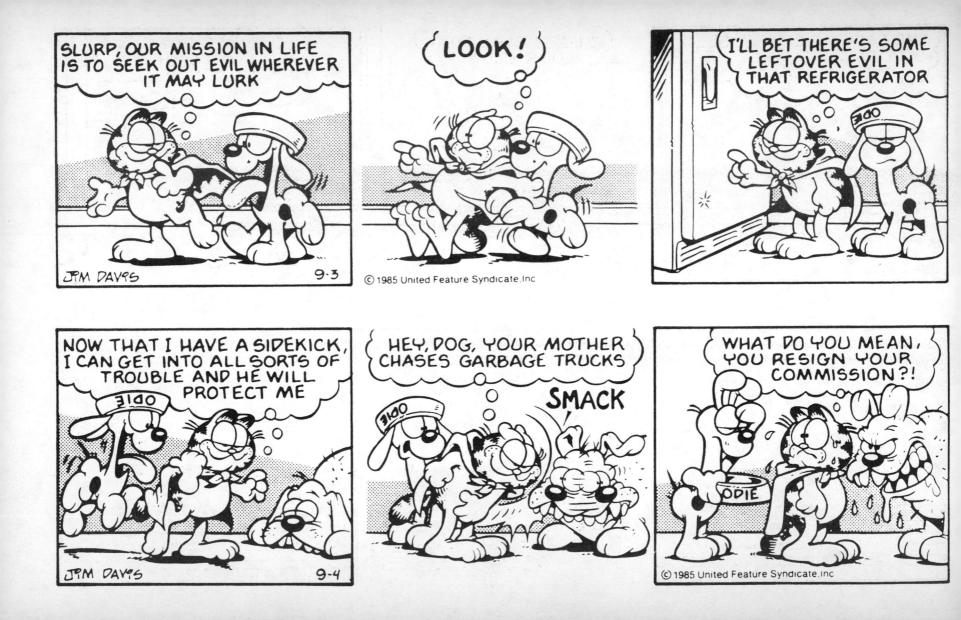

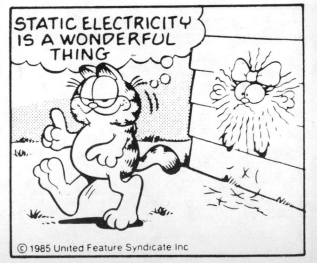

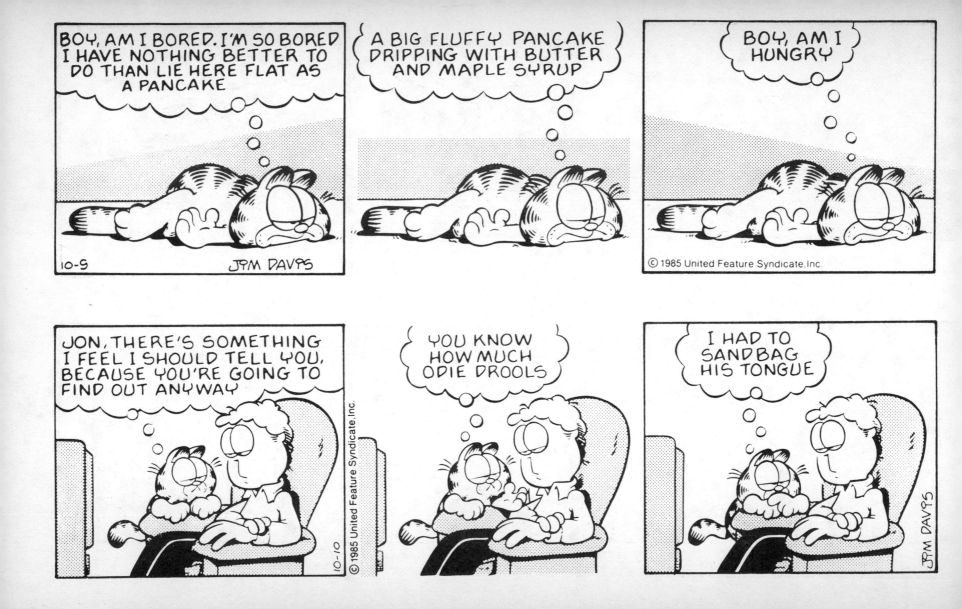

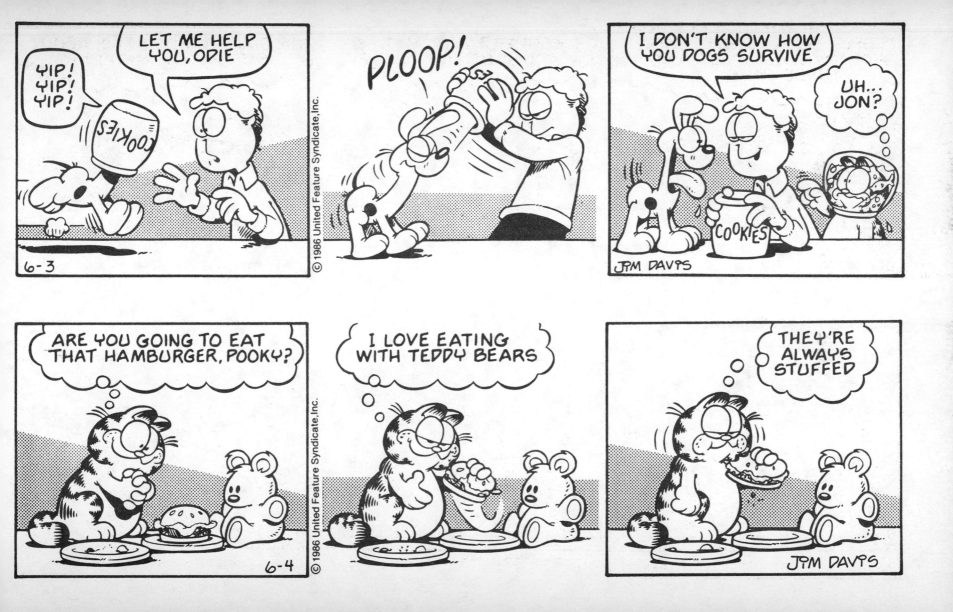

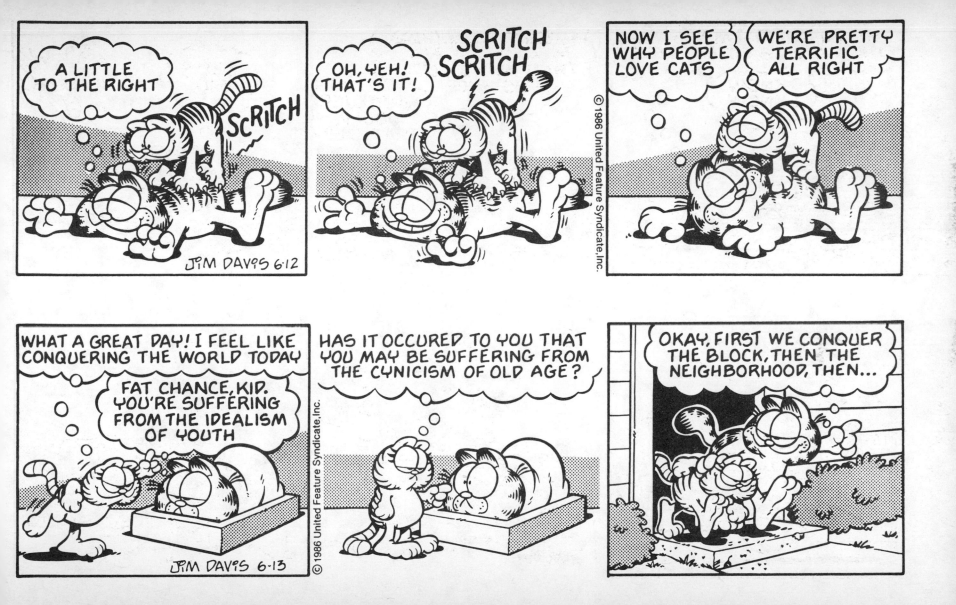

Other Garfield books published by Ravette

Garfield TV Specials
Here Comes Garfield	£2.95
Garfield On The Town	£2.95
Garfield In The Rough	£2.95
Garfield In Disguise	£2.95
Garfield In Paradise	£2.95
Garfield Goes To Hollywood	£2.95

Garfield Landscapes
Garfield The All-Round Sports Star	£2.50
Garfield The Irresistible	£2.50
Garfield On Vacation	£2.50
Garfield Weighs In	£2.50
Garfield I Hate Monday	£2.50
Garfield Special Delivery	£2.50
Garfield The Incurable Romantic	£2.50
Garfield Another Serve	£2.50
Garfield Wraps It Up	£2.50
Garfield Sheer Genius	£2.50

Garfield Pocket-books
No. 1	Garfield The Great Lover	£1.95
No. 2	Garfield Why Do You Hate Mondays?	£1.95
No. 3	Garfield Does Pooky Need You?	£1.95
No. 4	Garfield Admit It, Odie's OK!	£1.95
No. 5	Garfield Two's Company	£1.95
No. 6	Garfield What's Cooking?	£1.95
No. 7	Garfield Who's Talking?	£1.95
No. 8	Garfield Strikes Again	£1.95
No. 9	Garfield Here's Looking At You	£1.95
No. 10	Garfield We Love You Too	£1.95
No. 11	Garfield Here We Go Again	£1.95
No. 12	Garfield Life and Lasagne	£1.95
No. 13	Garfield In The Pink	£1.95
No. 14	Garfield Just Good Friends	£1.95
No. 15	Garfield Plays It Again	£1.95
No. 16	Garfield Flying High	£1.95

The Second Garfield Treasury	£5.95
The Third Garfield Treasury	£5.95
The Fourth Garfield Treasury	£5.95

All these books are available at your local bookshop or newsagent, or can be ordered direct from the publisher. Just tick the titles you require and fill in the form below. Prices and availability subject to change without notice.

Ravette Limited, 3 Glenside Estate, Star Road, Partridge Green, Horsham, West Sussex RH13 8RA

Please send a cheque or postal order, and allow the following for postage and packing. UK: Pocket-books and TV Specials – 45p for one book plus 20p for the second book and 15p for each additional book. Landscape Series – 45p for one book plus 30p for each additional book. Treasuries – 85p for one book plus 60p for each additional book.

Name ....

Address ....

....